W9-AWN-742

A GIFT FOR:

_____

PRESENTED BY:

_____

KILLER HISTORY

KILLER HISTORY

A GRUESOME AND GRISLY TRIP THROUGH THE PAST

CLIVE GIFFORD

Reader's Digest

The Reader's Digest Association, Inc.

New York, NY/Montreal

A READER'S DIGEST BOOK

Copyright © Buster Books 2012

First published in Great Britain in 2012 by Buster Books,
an imprint of Michael O'Mara Books Limited,
9 Lion Yard, Tremadoc Road, London SW4 7NQ

Library of Congress Cataloging in Publication Data

Gifford, Clive.
Killer history : a gruesome and grisly trip through the past / Clive Gifford.
pages cm
"First published in Great Britain in 2012 by Buster Books, an imprint of
Michael O'Mara Books Limited, 9 Lion Yard, Tremadoc Road, London."
Includes bibliographical references and index.
ISBN 978-1-62145-029-0 (alk. paper) -- ISBN 978-1-62145-031-3
(adobe : alk. paper) -- ISBN 978-1-62145-032-0 (epub : alk. paper)
1. World history--Miscellanea--Juvenile literature.
2. Death--History--Juvenile literature. I. Title.
D21.G46 2013
306.909--dc23
2012039971

We are committed to both the quality of our products and
the service we provide to our customers.
We value your comments, so please feel free to contact us.

The Reader's Digest Association, Inc.
Adult Trade Publishing
44 South Broadway
White Plains, NY 10601

For more Reader's Digest products and information, visit our website:
www.rd.com (in the United States)
www.readersdigest.ca (in Canada)

Printed in the United States of America

1 3 5 7 9 10 8 6 4 2

CONTENTS

ENTER AT YOUR OWN RISK . . .

Welcome to the most gory, gross, and downright gruesome collection of facts and stories about death, doom, and destruction!

From mummies and murderers, accidents, and autopsies, to blood, bones, and body bits, this bountiful book of death has it all, but be warned, it's not for the fainthearted.

There are hundreds of facts and haunting tales to freak out your friends, plus dead cool things you can make. If you come across a word you don't understand, check out the "Dreadfully Deadly Definitions" on page 138.

Are you brave enough to discover history's deadliest bits? Read this book if you dare. . . .

A DISAPPOINTING DEATH

In 1911, daredevil Bobby Leach sailed over the gigantic Niagara Falls in New York in a barrel and survived.

He went on to perform many other death-defying stunts.

However, in 1926, he died after slipping on a piece of orange peel.

FEET FIRST

In the 19th century, a dead person was usually carried out of the house feet first. This was to stop the spirit from looking back into the house and calling another member of the family to come with him or her.

Photographs or paintings of family members were also placed facedown or covered so that the dead person could not possess them.

EIGHT MORBID MUSEUMS

If you find yourself on a wet day with nothing weird to do, check out one of these monstrous museums.

1. The Museum of Funeral Carriages, Barcelona, Spain.

2. The Torture Museum, Amsterdam, The Netherlands.

3. The National Museum of Funeral History, Houston, Texas.

4. The Museum of Death, Hollywood, California.

5. The Mummy Museum, Guanajuato, Mexico.

6. The Medieval Torture Museum, San Gimignano, Italy.

7. The London Dungeon, London, England.

8. The Vienna Undertakers' Museum, Vienna, Austria.

THIS LINE IS KILLING ME!

ANCIENT ROMAN SITES

In ancient Rome, when someone died, a number of rituals were performed before the body was taken from the home and buried or cremated.

1. A family member, often the eldest son, performed the *conclamatio*—leaning over the body and calling the dead person's name to make sure he or she was really dead and not just pretending.

2. The eyes of the dead person were then closed.

3. The body was washed with warm water, and the legs and arms were straightened out.

4. If the deceased held an important position in the Roman Empire, a wax impression of the face was taken so that a sculpture could be made later.

5. The body was dressed in a toga and placed on a funeral couch with flowers around it.

6. Branches from mountain pine or cypress trees were pushed into the ground outside the front door to let passersby know that someone had died.

7. In some cases, a coin was placed with the body, usually in the mouth. This was to pay Charon, the ferryman. In Roman mythology, he was the god who transported dead Romans across the River Styx to Orcus, the Underworld.

MAKE A MUMMY IN EIGHT SIMPLE STEPS

Throughout history, people have had different ideas about what to do with the bodies of people who have died. One method that was especially popular in ancient Egypt was to mummify dead friends or relatives, to keep them fresh as a daisy for all eternity. Here's how they did it:

1. First, you have to get the body ready for "embalming"—preserving the flesh, so it doesn't rot away. You'll need a long hook, a knife, some salt called natron, some canopic jars to store the body parts in, and a strong stomach!

2. Start by pushing the hook into the nose of the body, toward the brain. The hook should help you to break up the brain matter, so you can pull it out through the nostril.

3. Take the knife and cut a slit in the side of the body to get to the organs.

4. Pull out the lungs, liver, stomach, and intestines,

but leave the heart (the Egyptians believed the dead would need it later). Use the natron to dry the organs and store each one in a separate canopic jar.

A cat amulet

5. Pack natron in and around the body and leave it to dry for 40 days.

6. While you are waiting, you might use your time effectively by choosing some amulets to wrap up with the body.

7. Once the body is dry and odor-free, you need to stuff it with linen, sawdust, herbs, spices, and more natron, then sew up the gap.

8. Now get wrapping! Cover the body completely in bandages. You'll need to use several layers—place an amulet between each layer.

The body is now ready to be placed in a tomb.

CORPSE COMPANIONS

Ancient Egyptians were so fond of their pets that many would have their dead cats, dogs, monkeys, and tons of other animals mummified and buried in their own tombs.

Mummified pets that archaeologists have found include . . .

. . . a dog	. . . a crocodile
. . . a hippo	. . . a lizard
. . . a hawk	. . . a fish
. . . a gazelle	. . . a beetle
. . . an ibis (a bird)	. . . an antelope.

A QUEEN WITH NO HEAD

Marie-Antoinette was not an everyday queen. She arrived in France at the age of 14 and was married to the future king.

Just a few years later, her husband became King Louis XVI, and Marie-Antoinette was queen. Not too happy with Louis, she distracted herself with the most frivolous and expensive activities she could find. Unfortunately, this didn't go down well with ordinary people, who hadn't been fond of the young queen in the first place.

Many people in France were extremely poor, and Marie-Antoinette became known as Madame Deficit, meaning that they blamed her for the country's debts.

In 1789, revolution broke out. People demanded an end to the monarchy, and the royal family was imprisoned. After a disastrous escape attempt, Louis was put on trial and beheaded in 1793.

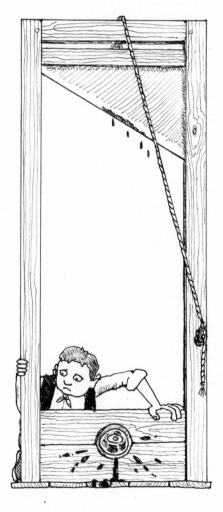

Marie-Antoinette went to the guillotine later that year and is said to have apologized for stepping on the foot of the executioner.

LA GUILLOTINE

The guillotine was first used in France in 1792. The idea was that all people executed should be killed in the same way, no matter how rich or poor they were. It was last used in 1977, before the death penalty was banned in France.

MIND-BOGGLING BOG PEOPLE

Some bogs (wet, marshy places) in colder parts of northern Europe are great at preserving dead bodies. There are lots of reasons for this, from the lack of oxygen in a bog (oxygen helps the body rot away) to some bogs being acidic and helping to "pickle" and preserve a body.

Tollund Man

This 2,400-year-old bog body is so well preserved that you can see all of his facial features. Experts think he was killed by being hanged, as a rope was still around his neck when his body was discovered in Denmark in 1950.

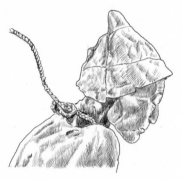

Clonycavan Man

This bog body, found in Ireland in 2003, was examined by Irish police experts. It seems he was murdered, possibly by an axe, about 2,300 years ago.

Yde Girl

Another murder victim, this 2,200-year-old bog body was found in the Netherlands. She was strangled and stabbed as a teenager.

Koelbjerg Woman

Found in a Danish bog, she is the oldest known bog person. She died more than 10,000 years ago but was only 20 to 25 when she died. Her body lay in water after death, so it wasn't mummified, but later the bog preserved her bones.

TOWER TERRORS

If you were locked up in the Tower of London, in England, in the times of the Tudors (1485–1603), then you had every reason to be terrified. Only a small number of important prisoners were sent there by the king or queen, but some never left the tower alive. During King Henry VIII's reign, 69 people imprisoned in the tower were executed.

WAYS TO TEST A WITCH

In medieval times, any woman who happened to live by herself and enjoy a little gardening might be suspected of being a witch. If she had an unpleasant wart or mole, then she was in real trouble. Here are some of the methods used to decide if someone was a witch:

Pricking the Flesh
A suspicious-looking wart or mole would be pricked with a needle. If it bled, the "witch" was innocent.

Scales of Justice

The accused woman would be weighed against a Bible—if she was heavier, she was certainly evil.

Ducking

The "witch" would be tied to a device called a ducking stool and plunged into water. If she floated, she was guilty and would be burned to death—if she drowned, she was innocent (but still dead!).

BOX TOXIC

Beautiful but oh-so-deadly, the box jellyfish (also called a sea wasp) has up to 60 tentacles, each covered in around 5,000 stinging cells, called nematocysts. The venom these contain is deadly. Just 0.1 ounces (3 grams) of the stuff would be enough to kill 60 humans. Since records were first kept in the 1950s, there have been more than 5,500 reported human deaths from box jellyfish stings.

ANIMALS ASSOCIATED WITH DEATH

Vulture

Owl

Crow

Moth

Bat

Cat

Raven

THE CIVIL WAR

The Civil War (1861–1865) is the deadliest war to have taken place in North America. It was fought between two sides, known as the Confederacy and the Union. It is now thought that around 750,000 people died during the conflict, but not necessarily because they killed one another!

As many as three out of five deaths on the Union side were said to be from disease rather than battle injuries.

According to official records, 64 Union soldiers were executed by the Confederate forces after being captured. But the sun posed a higher risk—313 Union soldiers died of sunstroke during the war.

QUICK, MEN, BREAK OUT THE SUNBLOCK!

THREE ENORMOUS EXPLOSIVE ERUPTIONS

Mount Tambora, Indonesia, 1815
Death toll: *more than 92,000 people*
Ten thousand were killed by the explosion itself, which blasted away over 3,300 feet (1,000 meters) of the top of the mountain. So much ash was thrown up into the atmosphere that 1816 was the coldest year in centuries over the whole planet. Crops failed, food was short, and thousands more people died.

Mount Pelée, West Indies, 1902
Death toll: *up to 40,000 people*
The eruption destroyed the entire city of St. Pierre as well as ships moored in the harbor and sailing nearby.

Mount Krakatoa, Indonesia, 1883
Death toll: *around 36,000 people*
More than half the island of Krakatoa was destroyed by the eruption, which could be heard in Australia, more than 2,000 miles (3,000 kilometers) away.

FATAL FOG

In the winter of 1952, "smog"—a lethal mixture of fog and harmful chemicals from coal fires and traffic—descended on the streets of London, England. It was so thick that traffic had to stop, and over the next few days, at least 4,000 people died from accidents or from breathing in the poisonous fumes.

AWFUL AUTOPSIES

An autopsy, also known as a post-mortem examination, is an investigation of a corpse carried out by a "pathologist"—a doctor skilled at figuring out how a person died.

> THIS ONE SEEMS TO HAVE KILLED HIM.

I Come to Examine Caesar
In 44 BCE, a Roman doctor named Antistius examined the body of murdered Roman leader Julius Caesar. He reported a whopping 23 stab wounds and pinpointed the fatal one.

Off and On
King Charles I of England was beheaded in 1649 and then had his head sewn back on before being buried.

In 1813, his body underwent an autopsy by the royal surgeon, Sir Henry Halford. Once again, the unfortunate king lost part of his anatomy, as Halford kept the fourth vertebra (part of his spine) and liked to shock guests with it at dinner parties.

Getting It in the Neck

Twelve days after he assassinated President Abraham Lincoln, John Wilkes Booth was shot in the back of the neck and killed. During his autopsy, three of his neck vertebrae had to be removed to reach the bullet.

These bones are now on display at the National Museum of Health and Medicine in Washington, DC. A rod shows the path of the bullet through the bones . . . if you're interested.

FASCINATING!

TOP TEN TERRIBLE TORTURES

Torture has been used throughout history to force people to say things they don't want to, or simply to punish them. The following terrible tortures tended to end in death. Unfortunate victims could be . . .

. . . covered with honey and left for insects to eat.

. . . stretched on a torture device called the rack until every joint was dislocated.

. . . tied to a large wheel and beaten to death.

. . . put inside an "iron maiden"—a metal suit full of spikes and blades.

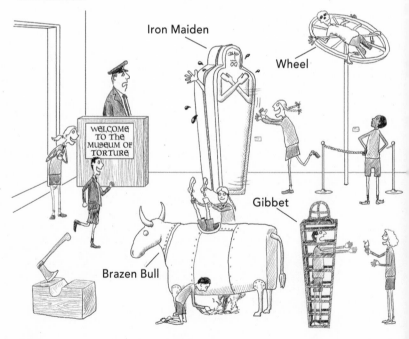

Iron Maiden

Wheel

WELCOME TO THE MUSEUM OF TORTURE

Gibbet

Brazen Bull

. . . cooked inside a metal container shaped like an animal—the brazen bull.

. . . seated with two spiked pieces of wood, called the knee splitter, that were slowly tightened around the knee (you can guess what happened).

. . . gibbeted (left to rot in an iron cage).

. . . lashed with a metal-spiked whip.

. . . placed in a skull crusher, which squeezed the head until the teeth broke and the brains squished out.

. . . tied up over bamboo shoots, which slowly and painfully grew through the body.

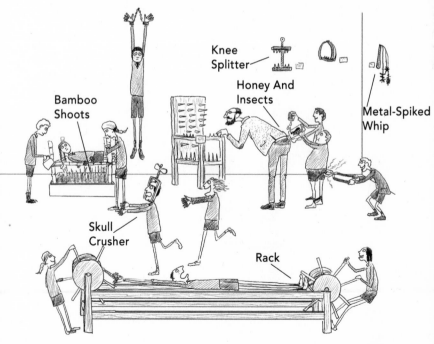

Knee Splitter

Honey And Insects

Metal-Spiked Whip

Bamboo Shoots

Skull Crusher

Rack

FASHIONS TO DIE FOR

We all know that fashion can be foolish as well as fun, but did you know that it can also be fatal?

Cruel Corsets

In the 19th and early 20th centuries, women in Europe and the United States wanted their waists to be as tiny as possible. They were laced with fearsome force into corsets strengthened with whalebone. Their inside organs were dangerously squeezed, and they could barely breathe—sometimes a life-threatening combination.

Joseph Hennella was an actor who pretended to be a woman. He became a true fashion victim when he collapsed on stage in St. Louis, Missouri, in 1912. His over-tight corset had caused breathing failure, and he died two hours later.

Flaming Hoops

Nineteenth-century ladies often wore vast skirts called crinolines. Huge hoops underneath made the skirts enormous, but they were also a major fire risk. Frances Appleton, the wife of a famous American poet named Henry Wadsworth Longfellow, was burned alive when her hooped skirt caught fire in 1861.

MMM . . . WHAT'S THAT YUMMY BARBECUE SMELL?

Doorway Disaster

In 1863, a fire in a large church in Santiago, Chile, turned into a disaster when women in hooped skirts couldn't squeeze through the exits fast enough. Their supersized skirts blocked the doorways, resulting in the deaths of between 2,000 and 3,000 people.

FATAL FACES

Lead Then Dead

Pale couldn't fail in the past, and for several centuries rich ladies covered their faces with white makeup called ceruse. This was an evil mixture of white lead and vinegar. The lead slowly poisoned the ladies' bodies, causing hair loss, rotting teeth, and eventually death.

I SAY, SHE'S A STUNNER!

Irish noblewoman Maria Gunning was just one would-be beauty who, in 1760, died of lead poisoning.

Beardy Weirdy

Male fashions could be just as lethal. In the 16th century, beards were all the rage. Hans Steininger was famous for having the longest beard in Austria— an incredible 51 inches (1.3 meters).

Unfortunately, when a fire broke out in 1567, Hans tried to flee but tripped over his beard, fell, broke his neck, and died.

Failing . . . and Falling

A tailor named Franz Reichelt fell to his death from the first deck of the Eiffel Tower, in Paris, France, in 1912. He was testing his new invention— an overcoat that worked as a parachute . . . or not, as it turned out.

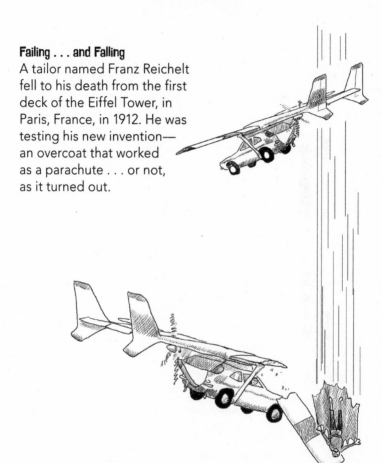

Up, Up and . . . Uh-Oh!

Henry Smolinski had a brilliant idea—a car that could fly! He died in 1973 when his AVE Mizar, a flying car based on a Ford Pinto, lost its right wing strut and crashed in California.

LIFE DETECTOR

A Danish surgeon named Jacob Winsløw (1669–1760) was worried that ways of deciding if someone was dead were not very reliable. Here are some of the suggestions he made for tests to make absolutely sure a person was deceased:

☠ Irritating the nose with onions and garlic

☠ Whipping the skin with stinging nettles

☠ Pushing long needles under the toenails

☠ Pulling the arms and legs violently

☠ Balancing a glass of water on the chest

☠ Pouring warm pee into the mouth

☠ Tickling the nose with a feather

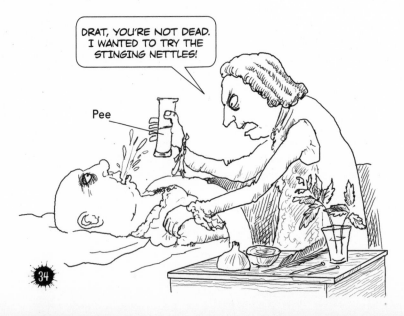

MUMMY POWDER

From the 12th century onward, a powder made by grinding up ancient Egyptian mummies was sold as a medicine that could cure almost anything.

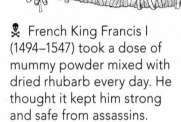

☠ French King Francis I (1494–1547) took a dose of mummy powder mixed with dried rhubarb every day. He thought it kept him strong and safe from assassins.

☠ King Charles II of England (1630–1685) often rubbed the powder on to his skin so he could absorb the ancient greatness of the pharaohs.

☠ Some artists added the powder to their paints, hoping it would give their artworks magical qualities.

☠ In the 17th and 18th centuries, demand for mummy dust was so high that crafty Egyptian merchants embalmed freshly dead people. Then they sold them as ancient mummies to foolish Europeans.

HOW TO SHRINK A HEAD

The Shuar tribe, and some other peoples living in the Amazon rainforest in South America, used to shrink the heads of enemies they had killed. Here's how they did it. **Warning:** This is seriously gross.

1. First kill your enemy— use any method you like except smashing the skull. Then cut off the head, including the neck.

2. Soak the head in hot water, and leave it for a few days to loosen the tissue. Make a slit in the back of the head and neck, and carefully peel the skin from the skull. Throw away the skull, or place it on a pole to scare people.

3. Scrape away the flesh inside the head and sew up the eyelids. Use tiny sticks or pins to close the lips.

4. Simmer the head for a couple of hours in boiling water and herbs, until it is one third of its original size and the skin is dark and rubbery.

5. Turn the skin inside out and scrape off any remaining flesh. Turn the skin the right way out again and sew up the slit at the back, leaving just an opening at the neck.

6. Heat some stones in a fire and drop them carefully inside the head to dry out the skin. Use hot sand in small areas, such as inside the nostrils.

7. Hang the head over a fire to harden and darken it. Give the hair a trim. If you like, add colored threads and beads to the head for decoration.

8. You will need to wear the head as a necklace or an accessory at three feasts to make sure its power passes to your tribe. After that, it makes a great decoration for your hut, or you could trade it for weapons to kill even more enemies.

Happy head shrinking!

WOW, COOL HEAD, MAN!

KILLER HISTORY

TILL DEATH DO US PART... OR NOT!

☠ When the wife of English knight Sir John Price died in the 17th century, he had her body embalmed. Each night, he slept in his bed beside her—even when he married his second wife!

☠ Queen Juana of Spain was devastated when her husband, Felipe, died. She kept his body in a coffin as she traveled from Belgium to Spain and often opened it up to kiss his very dead face.

KILLER HISTORY

💀 Prince Pedro of Portugal had bad luck with his wives. The third one, Inês de Castro, was murdered in 1355. Pedro tracked down the men who killed her and ripped out their hearts.

Legend has it that when he became king, he had her body dug up, then had her dressed in fine clothes and crowned as his queen. Some say his courtiers were forced to kiss her dead hand.

HOW TO MAKE A FAKE CAT MUMMY

First things first—never attempt this with a real cat. It's true that the ancient Egyptians mummified almost everything, including dung beetles, but they were particularly keen on mummifying kitties (see page 62).

Even in ancient times, though, there was tricky dealing. No one was likely to start unwrapping feline friends, so the embalmers often just bandaged up some random bones or bits of rags. Your fake cat mummy follows a fine tradition!

You Will Need:

• an empty plastic bottle • a bucket of soil or sand • newspaper • masking tape • a small piece of cardboard • glue • a paintbrush • cold, strong tea or coffee (no milk or sugar!) • bandages (strips of white cotton about 1 inch [3 centimeters] wide from an old sheet or pillowcase are fine, or narrow gauze bandages) • paint • felt-tip pens.

1. Put some soil or sand in the bottle to make it a bit heavier. Ball up some newspaper and push it into the neck of the bottle to make a head. Tape it in place with masking tape. Do the same with a smaller ball of newspaper to make the bottom round.

2. Make another small ball of newspaper and tape it to the front of the head. Cut two small ears from cardboard and tape those on as well.

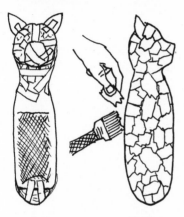

3. Mix some glue half-and-half with water. Tear up bits of newspaper, and glue them all over the mummy, covering up the bottle and masking tape. You will need at least two layers, and more on the head, to give a good cat shape. Let it dry out between layers.

4. Mix some glue with the cold, strong black tea or coffee to make a gloopy, dirty-looking mixture. Dip your bandage in it and start winding! Criss-cross the bandages on the final layer and tuck in the ends neatly.

Paint the head to match the body color and draw on the eyes and mouth.

DON'T BURY ME ALIVE!

In the past, many people were terrified of being assumed dead and buried while they were still very much alive. This fear even has a medical name: taphophobia (taf-oh-fo-be-ah). Some famous people chose weird ways to tackle their fear.

The Russian author Fyodor Dostoyevsky was so terrified of being assumed dead when he was just sleeping that he used to leave notes beside his bed when he went to sleep, assuring people that he was not dead.

More famously strange requests:

DO NOT LET MY BODY BE PUT INTO A VAULT LESS THAN TWO DAYS AFTER I AM DEAD.

MAKE THEM CUT ME OPEN, SO I WON'T BE BURIED ALIVE.

WHEN I'M DEAD, CUT OFF MY HEAD—JUST TO BE SURE.

George Washington (President)

Frédéric Chopin (Composer)

Harriet Martineau (Writer)

GREAT EXPECTATIONS

The last wish of famous author Charles Dickens was to have a very simple and private funeral and that no one who attended should wear a scarf, cloak, black bow, or "other such revolting absurdity." His funeral did take place with only close friends and family, but he was buried in Westminster Abbey in London, England. His grave was left open for several days so that thousands of people could pay their last respects.

TERRIBLE TYRANTS

Many rulers in the past were brutal, ruthless, and delighted by death. Here is a downright deadly collection of murderous monarchs, evil emperors, and rotten rulers.

Nasty Nero

The Roman emperor Nero liked to get rid of relatives. Maybe his murderous mother, Agrippina, had something to do with the way he turned out. She eliminated several of her son's rivals, but Nero didn't hesitate to kill her, too, when he had the chance, although it took several attempts.

Nero hired a serial killer, Locusta, to poison his brother Britannicus. He also tried to strangle his wife Octavia several times before having her veins cut so that she bled to death.

No Drinking Allowed!

The murderous Murad IV, sultan of the Ottoman Empire in the 17th century, made drinking coffee or alcohol in the city of Constantinople (in modern-day Turkey) a crime punishable by death. He sometimes performed the executions himself, using a giant weapon called a mace. He once had a group of dancing women put to death because they made too much noise.

THERE'S NOTHING LIKE A NICE CUP OF COFFEE.

NICE DAY AT THE OFFICE, DEAR?

Truly Terrible

A 16th-century ruler of Russia was known as Ivan the Terrible for a reason. He had thousands of enemies killed. Some were boiled alive, others had their arms and legs tied to four horses, which then galloped off in opposite directions. He even killed his own son by bashing him on the head with an iron-tipped staff.

WEIRD WILLS

Some people like to be in control—even when they're dead. Their last will and testament gives them one final chance to influence their nearest and dearest.

Beware of Hair
Henry Budd had 200,000 pounds when he died in 1862—a large fortune at the time. All the wealth was left to his two sons—providing neither grew a mustache.

STOP YOUR CRYING!

No Tears, Please!
Italian lawyer Ludovico Cortusio's will insisted that no one must weep at his cheerful funeral in 1418. If anyone did, they would find that they inherited a less-than-funny nothing at all.

Deathless Dummy
Famous ventriloquist Edgar Bergen left $10,000 to his dummy, Charlie McCarthy, to keep him in good condition. Charlie is now in the Smithsonian Institute in Washington, DC.

A Quiet Life
In 1929, Californian businessman John Quincy Murray left money to two of his granddaughters—as long as they never wore jewelry or makeup, never cut their hair short, did not wear short or low-cut dresses, and never went out to the movies or dances.

Rock On!
Rock singer Janis Joplin left $2,500 in her will to pay for an all-night party in California.

Holy Smoke!
Samuel Bratt's wife wouldn't allow him to smoke cigars. When he died in 1960, he bequeathed her 330,000 pounds— as long as she smoked five cigars a day.

PET PALS

Some wealthy people become so close to their pets that they leave money in their wills for their pooches and pussycats to be well looked after.

A Doggy Dynasty

German countess Carlotta Liebenstein left her entire $80 million estate to her pet dog, an Alsatian called Gunther III. After Gunther III died, the estate, now worth more than $200 million, passed on to another dog, Gunther IV. The pampered pooch lives with his own personal maid and chauffeur.

One Fabulous Feline
A stray cat called Tommaso became the world's richest kitty when his owner, Italian millionaire Maria Assunta, left her entire fortune of more than $15 million to him in 2011.

A Hand-Fed Hound
Business tycoon Leona Helmsley left her pet dog around $12 million in her will, but her relatives went to court to overturn her wishes. The Maltese terrier, whose name was Trouble, still ended up a millionaire, being awarded $2 million. His food was brought to him on a silver tray, and each morsel was hand-fed to him!

AVALANCHE!

There are an estimated one million avalanches around the world every year. Most are small and unnoticed. Some have been real killers.

☠ In 1910, trains pulling into Stevens Pass in Washington were prevented from traveling farther by heavy snow. While they waited, the trains were hit by a sudden avalanche, which swept the cars off a 130-foot-high (40-meter) cliff, killing 96 people.

It was the worst avalanche disaster ever in the United States.

💀 On September 4, 1618, the Rodi avalanche destroyed the Swiss town of Plurs and buried 2,427 people alive. None survived.

💀 During World War I, the armies of Austria and Italy fought each other through the mountains called the Alps. In December 1916, shots fired into shifting snow triggered a series of avalanches that killed between 9,000 and 10,000 troops from both armies.

💀 More than 2,200 years earlier, in 218 BCE, General Hannibal of Carthage led a giant army over the Alps on his way to attack the Romans in Italy. An avalanche wiped out around 18,000 of his men and about 2,000 of the army's horses, as well as most of its elephants.

KILLER HISTORY

LAST REQUESTS

☠ Magician and escapologist Harry Houdini's last request was for his wife, Bess, to hold a séance (a meeting to try to get in touch with the spirits of dead people) each year at Halloween, using ten secret words found in his will to try to contact him.

☠ The famous French general and leader Napoléon Bonaparte died in 1821. His last request asked for his head to be shaved and bits of his hair given to his friends.

I'M AFRAID MR. HOUDINI IS TIED UP AT THE MOMENT.

☠ Ancient Greek poet Virgil's last request was for his epic poem *The Aeneid* to be burned. Fortunately for lovers of poetry, his family didn't do what he asked, and the poem survived.

☠ T. M. Zink was a male lawyer who disliked women. When he died in 1930, he left $50,000 to build a womanless library, which would have no books by female authors and which women would not be allowed to enter. Members of Zink's family challenged his will successfully, and the library was never built.

☠ Writer Hunter S. Thompson got his last request—for his ashes to be fired out of a cannon perched on top of a tower more than 66 feet (20 meters) tall and shaped like a fist! The cannon was paid for by Hollywood actor Johnny Depp, who was a friend of Thompson's.

MASS-MURDERING MAN-EATERS

Some animals, when hungry or threatened, don't hesitate to attack and kill humans. Here is a short but savage list of some of the most terrible man-chomping creatures (and they wouldn't say no to eating women and children either).

☠ In 1898, a pair of male lions attacked and killed workers building a railway line and bridge across the Tsavo River in East Africa—not just once but over and over again. In a period of nine months, 135 workers were killed by the ferocious felines. Both were finally shot and killed. One of them was 10 feet (3 meters) long and needed eight men to carry him away.

☠ More than 60 years old, 20 feet (6 meters) long and weighing very nearly 1 ton (1,000 kilograms), a giant crocodile known as Gustave terrorized villagers in Burundi in Africa. He was last sighted in 2008. By then, he had attacked and killed more than 300 men, women, and children.

☠ A male leopard living in the Kumaon region of India killed more than 400 people before it was shot in 1910. It seems the leopard was injured and found it hard to catch and kill wild animals. Instead, it hunted humans.

☠ One female Bengal tiger became famous in the late 19th century when she killed 436 people in Nepal and India. The Champawat Tiger was finally shot and killed in 1907 by a big-game hunter named Jim Corbett.

DANCING WITH THE DEAD

Every five or seven years, some of the Malagasy people of Madagascar perform a funeral tradition called *Famadihana*, which means "the turning of the bones."

The ceremony involves digging up the bones of dead people, which are then sprinkled with perfume or wine and danced around, while elders tell stories about the dead people to younger members of the tribe. The bones are often wrapped in new shrouds before being returned to their graves.

MOUSE MURDER

If you had bad breath in ancient Egyptian times, you might look for mice to slice. One cure for bad breath at this time was to cut a mouse in two and place one half inside your mouth. Ugh!

DEADLY DINING

Even something as simple as chowing down on some dinner has been the end for certain people.

☠ An ancient Roman senator, Lucius Fabius Cilo, is said to have died during dinner after choking on a single hair that was found in his milk.

☠ American author Sherwood Anderson died in Panama in 1941 after swallowing part of a toothpick, which punctured a hole in his digestive system.

☠ Pope Clement VII died in 1534 after eating a highly poisonous death cap mushroom. No one knows if it was an accident or something more sinister.

☠ The parents of famous scientist and thermometer inventor Daniel Fahrenheit both died on August 14, 1701, after eating mushrooms that turned out to be poisonous.

☠ King Henry I of England died in 1135 of food poisoning, after eating far too many stewed lampreys—eel-like creatures thought tasty at the time. He died while in France, so his remains were sewn into the skin of a bull and shipped back to England to be buried.

PRETTY NAUGHTY POLLY

In 1845, at the funeral of Andrew Jackson, the seventh president of the United States, it is said that his pet parrot, Pol, attended. The bird had to be removed from the ceremony when he started swearing in English and Spanish. Could he have learned these rude words from the president?

FEARSOME PHOBIAS

Coimetrophobia (coy-met-ro-fo-be-ah)—fear of cemeteries
Myctophobia (mic-to-fo-be-ah)—fear of darkness
Necrophobia (nec-ro-fo-be-ah)—fear of death or dead things
Phasmophobia (fas-mo-fo-be-ah)—fear of ghosts
Placophobia (plak-oh-fo-be-ah)—fear of tombstones
Tomophobia (to-mo-fo-be-ah)—fear of surgical operations

DEATH OF A PRESIDENT

Eight presidents have died in office. Seven of them were elected in a year ending in zero, and the other one died in a year ending in zero. Weird!

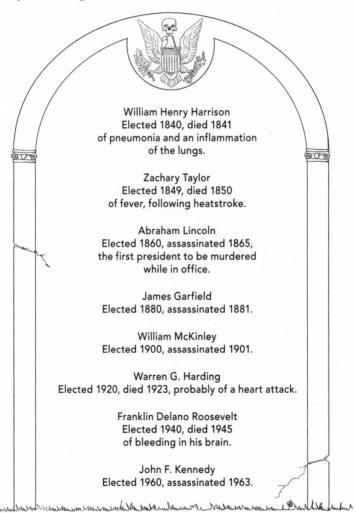

William Henry Harrison
Elected 1840, died 1841
of pneumonia and an inflammation
of the lungs.

Zachary Taylor
Elected 1849, died 1850
of fever, following heatstroke.

Abraham Lincoln
Elected 1860, assassinated 1865,
the first president to be murdered
while in office.

James Garfield
Elected 1880, assassinated 1881.

William McKinley
Elected 1900, assassinated 1901.

Warren G. Harding
Elected 1920, died 1923, probably of a heart attack.

Franklin Delano Roosevelt
Elected 1940, died 1945
of bleeding in his brain.

John F. Kennedy
Elected 1960, assassinated 1963.

OOPS!

Is this the worst luck ever? In 1794, the crew of the *Jackal* fired a 13-gun salute in honor of John Kendrick, a famous sea captain and explorer. Kendrick was moored close by in his boat, the *Lady Washington*. One of the cannons was accidentally loaded with real shot instead of blanks, which hit and killed Kendrick outright.

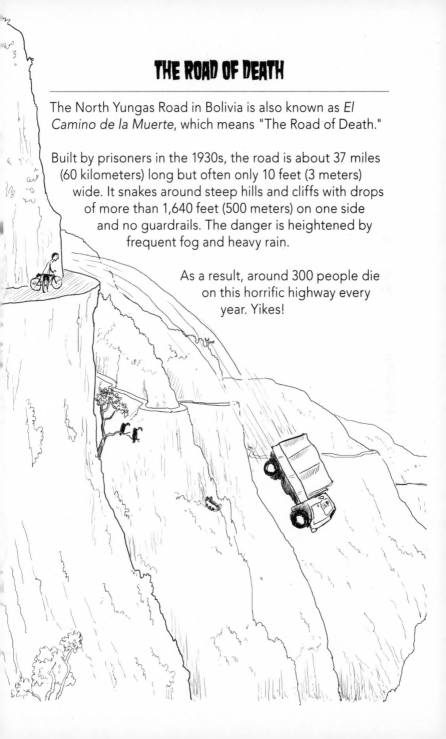

THE ROAD OF DEATH

The North Yungas Road in Bolivia is also known as *El Camino de la Muerte*, which means "The Road of Death."

Built by prisoners in the 1930s, the road is about 37 miles (60 kilometers) long but often only 10 feet (3 meters) wide. It snakes around steep hills and cliffs with drops of more than 1,640 feet (500 meters) on one side and no guardrails. The danger is heightened by frequent fog and heavy rain.

As a result, around 300 people die on this horrific highway every year. Yikes!

PET MATTERS

It wasn't only the ancient Egyptians who were fond of their pets (see page 40 for some mummified kitties). Animal lovers throughout history have grieved when their pets passed away.

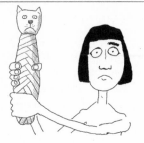

☠ Alexander the Great (356–323 BCE) owned a dog called Peritas. It is said that when she died, he led a large funeral procession to her grave, erected a stone monument, and ordered those who lived nearby to celebrate her memory every year.

☠ Cyrus the Great (580–529 BCE) was a king of ancient Persia. He got so upset when one of his favorite horses drowned that he sentenced the offending river to "death." A tricky execution to carry out? Not at all. Cyrus had channels dug so that the river drained to a shallow depth in which no horse could drown.

I DON'T THINK THIS IS WORKING, SIRE.

☠ When Pope Leo X's favorite pet, Hanno, died in 1516 he was buried in the Belvedere courtyard in the Vatican in Rome, Italy. The Pope wrote a poem about his lost pet and also commissioned the famous painter Raphael to paint a series of scenes commemorating Hanno's life. Hanno was an elephant!

☠ The *Cimetière des Chiens*, a pet cemetery, opened in Paris, France, in 1899. More than 40,000 pets are buried there. The most famous is Rin Tin Tin, a dog who starred in 26 Hollywood films before his death in 1932. The *Cimetière des Chiens* may not be the oldest pet cemetery though. Recent archaeological digs at Ashkelon in Israel revealed a dog cemetery that dates back more than 2,000 years.

EXPIRING EXPLORERS

Exploration has always been a risky business. When brave (sometimes foolhardy) adventurers set off into the unknown, some of them are almost certain not to come back.

Captain James Cook
This famous British sea captain had mapped much of Australia's eastern coast and parts of the Pacific Ocean, and lived to tell the tale. In 1779 he went back to Kealakekua Bay in the Hawaiian Islands for ship repairs, where fights broke out and he was killed. As a mark of respect, local chiefs cooked his body so that his bones could be cleaned and kept.

David Livingstone
In 1883, Livingstone, a Scottish explorer of parts of central Africa, died in the village of Ilala in modern day Zambia from malaria and internal bleeding caused by truly dreadful diarrhea. Yuck!

Juan de la Cosa

This Spanish sailor made some of the first maps of the coastline of the Americas. He was killed in Cartagena, Colombia, in 1509, by poison darts and arrows fired by hostile locals.

OW! DARN MOSQUITOES!

Burke and Wills

Robert Burke and William Wills headed an ill-fated expedition to cross Australia from south to north. The explorers took with them more than 200 pounds (90 kilograms) of soap, 1.4 tons (1,300 kilograms) of sugar, 400 pounds (180 kilograms) of bacon, and a Chinese dinner gong. Somehow, the pair managed to die of starvation on the way back from northern Australia in 1861.

I WISH WE HADN'T EATEN IT ALL IN THE FIRST WEEK.

WE'VE STILL GOT THE SOAP.

Robert de La Salle

La Salle was a French explorer who traveled around the Great Lakes of North America and parts of the southern United States. In 1687, while he was exploring what is now Texas, some members of his expedition turned against him and shot him dead.

HOT STUFF

According to legend, ancient Roman general Marcus Licinius Crassus was killed in around 53 BCE by the Parthians from ancient Persia, who poured molten gold down his corpse's throat—as a symbol of the general's greed.

CREATIVE COFFINS

The Ga-Adangbe people from the West African nation of Ghana are famous for their fancy funerals. They make coffins that match the dead person's interests or requests. Coffins have been made in the shape of . . .

. . . a mobile phone
. . . a taxi cab
. . . a large fish
. . . a lion
. . . a crab
. . . a pineapple
. . . an airliner
. . . a soda bottle
. . . a peacock
. . . a sneaker.

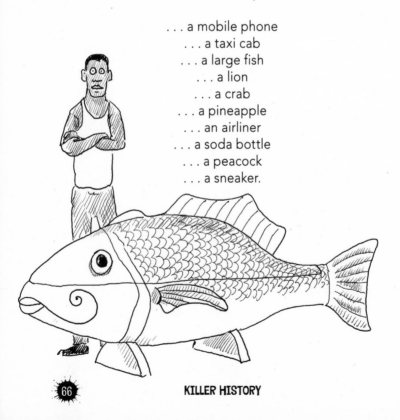

FAMOUS LAST WORDS

"Go away. I'm all right."
(H. G. Wells, science-fiction author, 1946)

"Don't let it end like this! Tell them I said something!"
(Pancho Villa, Mexican revolutionary, to a nearby journalist
as he died from a bullet wound, 1923)

"Am I dying, or is this my birthday?"
(Lady Astor, seeing her bed surrounded by relatives, 1964)

"They couldn't hit an elephant at this dist—"
(General John Sedgwick, misjudging the aim of
Confederate soldiers he was fighting in the Civil War, 1864)

HOW TO TAKE A BRASS RUBBING

Many tombs and monuments to dead people have words and pictures engraved on them, either on brass plates or on the stone itself. You can make a copy of these by laying a piece of paper on them and rubbing over them gently with a crayon.

You Will Need:

• a soft brush or cloth • strong but thin paper
• masking tape • wax crayons
• permission from the clergyperson or caretaker.

1. Use the soft brush or cloth to clear the surface of dust or grit that might tear the paper.

2. Place the paper over the words or pictures, and use masking tape to make sure it can't move.

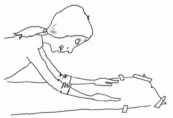

3. Using the long side of the crayon, rub very gently over the object in one direction until all the engraving shows on the paper.

4. Remove the masking tape slowly and carefully, and lift the paper away.

☠ Experiment with colors. Gold or white crayon on black paper is good.

FIT FOR A DEAD QUEEN

Emperor Shah Jahan ordered an amazing tomb for his wife Mumtaz Mahal, who died giving birth to the couple's fourteenth child in 1631. It took 22 years and 20,000 workers to complete it, and the Taj Mahal, in Agra, India, is one of the world's most famous and beautiful buildings. It is, however, not certain that Mumtaz is actually buried there.

SCARED OF THE DARK

Emperor Louis the Pious was the son of a man named Charlemagne, king of the Franks. In 840, the sky became totally dark in the daytime, during a solar eclipse. Five minutes later, daylight returned, but according to legend, Louis didn't. He had died of fright.

VIOLENT VESUVIUS

On a summer morning in 79 CE, people who lived in and near the town of Pompeii on the Italian coast woke up as usual. Within hours, their world split apart when the mountain that stood behind the town blasted into horrific life.

Before the massive eruption, there had been signs of approaching disaster, such as small earthquakes. But local people didn't know Vesuvius was a volcano. It hadn't erupted for 1,800 years. They didn't even have a word in Latin for "volcano."

No one was killed by red hot lava gushing down the slopes of Vesuvius. There wasn't any. Instead, super-heated gas, "magma" (molten rock), and ash rose high into the air, where it cooled—then fell as ash and rock.

Pompeii was buried in the hot ash, killing many people instantly.

Archaeologists have worked to uncover this buried town, which was preserved by the ash that covered it. The remains of people and even animals have been discovered, frozen where they fell thousands of years ago.

KILLER HISTORY

MAKE YOUR OWN VOLCANO

You Will Need:

- a tray • modeling clay, papier-mâché, or soil
- a plastic bottle or container
- 1–2 tablespoons bicarbonate of soda (baking soda)
- red food dye • liquid soap • ⅛ cup (30 milliliters) vinegar.

1. Build a cone-shaped volcano on the tray. You can make this from modeling clay, papier-mâché, or soil from the garden. Leave an opening in the middle, big enough for your plastic container to fit inside.

2. Put the bicarbonate of soda (baking soda) and a few drops of food dye into your plastic container. Add three or four drops of liquid soap. Fill up the bottle with warm water, but leave space for the vinegar.

3. Put the bottle in the middle of your volcano and quickly pour in the vinegar in one shot. Stand back and watch the volcano erupt. The vinegar and bicarbonate of soda react with each other to make carbon dioxide gas. Red "lava" should bubble up and run down the sides of your erupting volcano.

DANGER SIGNS

Deadly chemicals are transported all over the world by air, road, rail, and sea. In case of an accident, it's important that the emergency services know what they're dealing with. International symbols have been developed so that anyone, anywhere can be forewarned.

Danger: may catch fire

Danger: highly poisonous

Danger: may harm the environment

Danger: may seriously harm health

Danger: gas under pressure

Danger: explosive material

Danger: may cause health difficulties

Danger: may cause or worsen fire

Danger: corrosive (may burn what it touches)

IT'S NUTS!

More people are killed each year by coconuts falling on their heads than by sharks.

THE MAN WITH TWO HEADS

Famous classical composer Joseph Haydn died in 1809 and was buried in Hundsturm Cemetery on the outskirts of Vienna, Austria. Shortly after his funeral, two men, Joseph Rosenbaum and Johann Peter, broke into Haydn's grave and cut off his head. They were enthusiastic "phrenologists"—people who think that studying the bumps on someone's head can give clues to his or her personality.

The daring duo hid the head under a straw mattress but found themselves under suspicion. When questioned, Rosenbaum gave the authorities a different head, which was then buried with Haydn's headless body.

Haydn's real head wasn't reunited with his body until 1954. Both heads were put on display in Eisenstadt in Austria in 2009 to mark the 200th anniversary of his death.

COLORS OF MOURNING

In many Western countries, people traditionally wear black clothes after someone close to them has died, to show that they are in mourning for their loved one. But in some cultures, it's all about the color!

☠ In South Africa, people wear red clothes to funerals, as this color is associated with sadness and loss.

☠ Rather than wearing white to a wedding, Japanese mourners dress in white clothes when someone has died. Often they wear a white carnation, too.

☠ Purple is the traditional color of mourning in Thailand—but not for everybody. Widows mourning their husbands can be seen wearing purple.

☠ Although it might seem bright and sunny, in Egypt and Myanmar it's yellow that is associated with death and mourning, and is the suitable color to wear to a funeral.

EINSTEIN'S BRILLIANT BRAIN

When it comes to smart people, few are thought of as brainier than the brilliant scientist Albert Einstein. When he died in 1955, his brain was removed by Thomas Harvey, who weighed it as 2.7 pounds (1.23 kilograms).

Some of the brain was cut into thin slices to be examined on microscope slides, but Harvey kept the rest of the brain in a jar at home. The brain survived many house moves before finally being given to Princeton University.

BODY SNATCHERS!

Medical students and researchers learn a lot by "dissecting"—cutting up—dead bodies. In the past, medical schools paid good money for bodies and sometimes didn't ask too many questions.

☠ Four medical students in the Italian city of Bologna were caught digging up the recently buried body of a criminal as long ago as 1319.

☠ In the 18th and 19th centuries, hundreds of bodies were snatched from the Bully's Acre Cemetery in Dublin for Irish medical schools—perhaps as many as 2,000.

☠ In the 19th century, about 200 body snatchers were at work in London. In 1830–1831 alone, seven body-snatching gangs were caught by police.

NO, OFFICER, I'M JUST TAKING MY DEAR OLD MOTHER FOR A WALK.

William Burke and William Hare were notorious body snatchers in Edinburgh in the early 19th century, selling corpses to doctors and surgeons. When they struggled to find newly buried bodies, they started murdering people. Burke was found guilty of murder and hanged in 1829. Then his body was given to medical science for a taste of his own medicine.

THE DAY OF THE DEAD

All Saints' Day is on November 1 each year. In Mexico, this is known as *Dia de los Muertos* in Spanish—"Day of the Dead." It is a day when dead friends and family members are remembered.

Far from being sad or scary, this day is a celebration. People wear wooden skull masks called *calacas*, bring gifts to the dead people's graves, and dance in honor of their relatives.

Special food is made and eaten, such as sugary sweets in the shape of skulls and *pan de muerto*—"bread of the dead"—which may be decorated with small dough teardrops or bone shapes (see pages 118–119 to find out how to make your own). An altar is often made in the home and decorated with candles and photos of the dead loved ones.

KILLER HISTORY

AN ARMY FOR A (DEAD) EMPEROR

In 1974, farmers in Xi'an, China, found the giant underground tomb of the first emperor of China, Qin Shi Huangdi. Qin Shi Huangdi spent much of his life trying to find an "elixir of life"—a medicine that would mean he would never die. He never found it, but took mercury to try to live longer. Mercury is poisonous so this is, in fact, probably what killed him.

The tomb is is full of amazing life-size statues, all made of terracotta—a kind of clay. It is said that they were made to guard and protect the emperor after death. There are probably 8,000 terracotta warriors in the tomb. Only a fraction have been excavated so far. There are also hundreds of statues of horses, chariots, and even acrobats.

In the earth, the statues are brightly colored. They turn grey when exposed to the air.

THE EMPEROR'S TIRED OF WARRIOR STATUES. BURY 'EM!

BODY PARTS AND PARTED BODIES

☠ For almost 30 years after the beheading of Sir Walter Raleigh in 1618, his wife, Elizabeth, kept his preserved head in a red leather bag.

I'M SURE MY KEYS ARE IN HERE SOMEWHERE . . . OOPS!

☠ The Wilder Brain Collection is a group of more than 70 whole brains of dead people, preserved and stored at Cornell University.

☠ In 2010, the Museum of the History of Science in Florence, Italy, displayed a tooth, a finger, and a thumb belonging to the great scientist and telescope pioneer Galileo. They were only discovered in 2009, when an art dealer, Alberto Bruschi, bought an old wooden case and found them inside.

☠ The bladder of Italian biologist Lazzaro Spallanzani, who died in 1799, is still on display in a room of medical exhibits at the University of Pavia in Italy.

WHAT DO YOU MEAN YOU'VE LOST IT?

☠ Badu Bonsu II of the Ahanta tribe (in present-day Ghana), was beheaded by Dutch soldiers in 1838. His head disappeared and was thought lost until more than 150 years later, when it was found pickled in a jar in a Dutch museum. In 2009, members of the Ahanta tribe flew from Africa to the Netherlands to take the head back to Ghana.

THE WORLD'S MOST MURDEROUS CREATURE

Is it a human? Is it a lion? Is it a shark? Nope! The mosquito takes the title of the most murderous creature. Mosquitoes carry the deadly disease malaria, which infects as many as 500 million people a year. Between 500,000 and 1,000,000 people die from the disease each year.

LETHAL LEISURE

No matter how innocent a pastime or hobby may seem, things can sometimes go wrong in the deadliest of ways.

An Audience Accident

Ancient Roman gladiators often fought to the death, but those watching them were sometimes in danger as well. In 27 BCE, an ancient Roman amphitheater collapsed in Fidenae, Italy. As many as 20,000 of the 50,000 audience members died.

The Show Must Go On

In 1958, a TV drama series was being filmed and transmitted live when one of the actors, Gareth Jones, died between scenes. Off camera, the director furiously scribbled on scripts, giving the actor's remaining lines to other cast members so that the show could continue to be broadcast.

KILLER HISTORY

I'M DYING OF BOREDOM HERE.

A Theatrical Murder
Abraham Lincoln was the first president to be assassinated.
He was shot in 1865, while watching a play at a theater in
Washington, DC.

Bullet Backfire
Chung Ling Soo was
known as "the marvelous
Chinese conjuror." He
wasn't Chinese at all, but
an American performer
who pretended he didn't
understand English. When
he was on stage in 1918,
his bullet-catching trick
went disastrously wrong,
and he died from a bullet
wound the next day.

SOMETHING'S GONE WRONG!

HE'S SPEAKING ENGLISH—WHAT A TRICK!

DEATH PENALTIES

Lethal Law

The first record of criminals being sentenced to death was found in the Code of King Hammurabi of Babylon, written more than 3,750 years ago. Crimes punishable by death included burglary and falsely accusing someone of a crime.

Killed by Kindness

In Athens, Greece, 2,700 years ago, a super-strict set of laws demanded death for many different crimes. The man who made these laws, Draco, is said to have died when grateful locals showered him with clothes and cloaks, suffocating him to death!

Beware, Bunny Burglars!

In Britain, by the 1700s, there were a staggering 222 different crimes that carried the death sentence. These included cutting down a tree, printing fake tax stamps, and robbing a rabbit hutch!

SERVES HIM RIGHT!

HE HASN'T LEARNED A THING!

Parsley Punishment

In 1612, the governor of British settlers in the Virginia Colony brought in strict new laws, including the death penalty for crimes such as stealing herbs or grapes, trading with Native Americans, and making "unseemly or unfitting speeches."

WEIRD WORLD WAR I WEAPON

The gigantic Paris Gun was a massive World War I weapon. It was more than 130 feet (40 meters) long, and the shells it fired each weighed a whopping 265 pounds (120 kilograms). The gun was so powerful that it was placed more than 62 miles (100 kilometers) from Paris, yet its shells reached the city, causing more than 250 deaths.

PARIS IS OVER THERE. YOU'VE JUST HIT BERLIN!

EVEN WEIRDER WORLD WAR II WEAPONS

☠ During World War II, the Soviet army tried to train dogs to carry anti-tank mines under German tanks. The plan was that the mine would blow up the enemy tank—and unfortunately the dog along with it. But things didn't exactly go as planned. When unleashed on the battlefield, many of the dogs simply ran away or headed for the nearest Soviet tanks!

. . . AND THEN YOU CRAWL UNDER THE GERMAN TANKS AND BLOW THEM UP.

YEAH, IN HIS DREAMS!

KILLER HISTORY

☠ The *Yokosuka MXY-7 Ohka* was a small, rocket-powered Japanese aircraft, designed as a flying bomb. Pilots would aim the plane at US warships. One such suicide mission helped to sink the warship USS *Mannert L. Abele.*

IS IT SUPPOSED TO BE COMING THIS WAY?

ARE YOU SURE THIS IS RIGHT?

☠The *Krummlauf*, meaning "curved barrel," was a bent gun barrel fitted to a German *Sturmgewehr 44* assault rifle—so that soldiers could shoot around corners!

☠ One truly wild American World War II plan was to drop lots of Mexican bats, each equipped with an "incendiary"—fire-causing—bomb, over the largely wooden cities of Japan. Timers would cause the bombs to explode after the bats had landed. Tests were carried out by the Air Force and Navy, but the batty plan never saw action.

I THINK WE SHOULD TRY A SMALLER BOMB.

KILLER HISTORY

DING-DONG, I'M NOT DEAD!

In the 19th century, many people were really afraid of being buried alive. Various ingenious ideas were designed to make sure people were truly dead when buried.

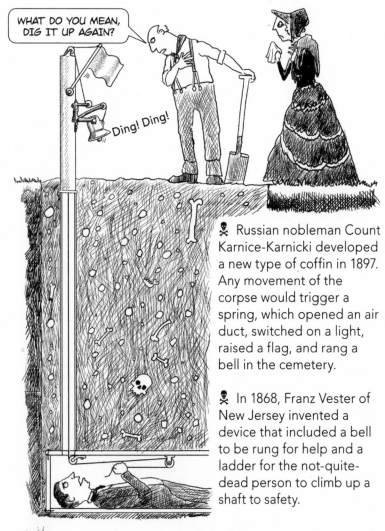

WHAT DO YOU MEAN, DIG IT UP AGAIN?

Ding! Ding!

☠ Russian nobleman Count Karnice-Karnicki developed a new type of coffin in 1897. Any movement of the corpse would trigger a spring, which opened an air duct, switched on a light, raised a flag, and rang a bell in the cemetery.

☠ In 1868, Franz Vester of New Jersey invented a device that included a bell to be rung for help and a ladder for the not-quite-dead person to climb up a shaft to safety.

☠ In the UK, William Tebb and others formed the Society for the Prevention of People Being Buried Alive. It encouraged people to bury crowbars, shovels, and bells in their graves so that if they happened to be alive, they could get out.

☠ In some parts of Germany in the 19th century, a simpler method was used. Dead people were laid out in a *Leichenhaus*—a "corpse house" or mortuary—and attached to a bell by wire. If a corpse moved, the bell rang. The grim job of the staff there was to wait a few days for any sign of life, then bury the definitely dead corpse. For a small fee in some mortuaries, members of the public could view the grisly scene.

ANIMAL ASSAULTS

Stranger Than Fiction

Aeschylus, an ancient Greek playwright, is said to have died in 456 or 455 BCE when an eagle flying high above dropped a tortoise on his head. It was extraordinarily bad luck for Aeschylus—and the tortoise.

HAH! THEY WILL SUSPECT NOTHING!

OH NO!

OH NO!

OH NO!

Violent Vermin

During World War II, members of the resistance network fighting Germany and its allies in Europe filled dead rats with explosives. The plan was to put the dead rats on piles of coal at railway stations so that when they were loaded into the boiler of a steam train, they would explode. However, the plan was foiled by the Germans the first time it was used.

Monkey Business

King Alexander I of Greece died in 1920 after being bitten by a monkey in the Royal Gardens in Athens, where he had been walking his dog. He died of an infection four weeks later.

I SAID THEY'D NEED STRONGER CHAINS.

Jumbo Justice

A circus elephant called Mary killed her new handler, Walter "Red" Eldridge, in 1916. She was executed for her crime—hanged from a large railway crane in Erwin, Tennessee—the very next day.

TAKE IT TO THE GRAVE

Some people have insisted on being buried with possessions that meant a lot to them in life.

☠ When 37-year-old oil heiress Sandra Ilene West died in 1977, she was buried in her blue 1964 Ferrari 330. The entire car was encased in a box buried at the Alamo Masonic Cemetery in Texas.

☠ Reuben John Smith was buried in 1899. He was seated in an oak and leather reclining chair, along with a warm coat and hat, and with a checkerboard on his lap.

☠ Queen Victoria was buried with the bathrobe of her long-dead husband, Prince Albert, as well as a plaster cast of his hand and a lock of the hair of her servant John Brown.

☠ Horror-film actor Bela Lugosi was buried in 1956 wearing the black cape he had worn in a number of *Dracula* films.

KILLER HISTORY

ON THE MOVE

Some bodies have been dug up and moved over and over again. The record must surely belong to President Abraham Lincoln, whose body has been moved a staggering 17 times.

NOT AGAIN!

☠ King Frederick the Great of Prussia asked to be buried at his palace of Sanssouci but was buried instead in a church in Potsdam, Germany, in 1786. In 1943, his body was moved first to Berlin and then to a salt mine to keep it safe during World War II. After the war, it was reburied in Hohenzollern Castle near Stuttgart. Finally, in 1991, he was reburied at his palace of Sanssouci.

☠ Eva Perón, the wife of the president of Argentina, died in 1952. Her body was preserved and was put on display in Argentina before it mysteriously disappeared. In 1971, it was revealed that it had been secretly taken to Italy and buried in Milan. The body was then moved to Spain, and in 1974, it returned to Argentina. That's a lot of air miles!

FIVE DEADLY PLACE NAMES

1. The Dead Sea, Israel and Jordan

Ten times saltier than the the world's oceans, this body of water deserves its name, as only a few bacteria are able to live there.

2. Death Valley, Arizona

Death Valley is North America's driest and hottest spot. In 1849, travelers heading for California's gold fields suffered two months of "hunger and thirst and an awful silence" there. As they left, one looked back and said, "Good-bye, Death Valley." The name stuck.

3. The Skeleton Coast, Namibia

This coast is littered with the bones of whales and the remains of shipwrecks. Vicious currents, fog, winds, and rocks make it a deadly place for animals and humans.

4. Tombstone, Arizona

This desert town sprung up because silver was discovered nearby. It soon got a reputation as one of the wildest places of the Wild West, and many cowboys and prospectors did end up in its cemeteries.

5. Murder Island, Nova Scotia, Canada

There are many different stories about the reasons for the name of this tiny island. Whichever is true, there is no doubt that in the last century, bleached human bones were often found on the stony beaches.

BRILLIANT LAST WORDS (MAYBE)

Albert Einstein, one of the most brilliant scientists who ever lived, mumbled a few words on his deathbed. They may have been amazing, but we'll never know. He spoke in his first language—German—and his American nurse didn't understand a word of it.

SERIOUSLY DANGEROUS SCIENCE

☠ Brilliant chemist Carl Scheele was the first to discover oxygen and also the first to identify the elements manganese, chlorine, and tungsten. He tended to taste his new discoveries, which may have been unwise, as he is believed to have died of mercury and lead poisoning in 1786.

☠ Georg Wilhelm Richmann was an early student of electricity. Unfortunately, while examining an electrical experiment during a storm in 1753, he was struck by lightning that traveled through his apparatus and killed him instantly.

☠ Nobel Prize–winning scientist Marie Curie spent much of her life working with radioactive materials. She died from leukemia, believed to have been caused by radiation exposure, in 1934.

☠ Russian revolutionary and doctor Alexander Bogdanov was experimenting with blood transfusions when, in 1928, he gave himself a transfusion of blood from a student who had malaria and tuberculosis. He died shortly afterwards.

☠ Famous scientist and thinker Francis Bacon died in 1626 after a pioneering attempt to preserve food by freezing it. He spent too long outside packing snow into a chicken, contracted pneumonia, and died a week later.

DUMB, DUMB DEATHS

☠ Attila the Hun was the most feared warrior of his age, but one story tells that he died in 453 CE on his wedding night (he already had several wives), after drinking too much alcohol. He suffered a nosebleed and, too drunk to notice, choked to death on the blood.

☠ Martin of Aragon ruled not only Aragon, in Spain, but the islands of Sardinia, Corsica, and Sicily, as well as being Count of Barcelona. In 1410, he is said to have died from a fatal laughing fit combined with very severe indigestion.

☠ Milo of Croton won wrestling competitions at five ancient Olympic Games and was renowned for his enormous strength . . . but not for his brains. Finding a tree trunk split with wedges, he put his hands into the gap to try to rip the trunk in two. Unfortunately, the wedges fell out, and Milo was trapped in the trunk. Unable to escape, he was devoured by a pack of wolves.

☠ Clement Vallandigham was a congressman and a lawyer. While defending Thomas McGehan on a charge of murder, Vallandigham showed the court how the gunshot could have been accidental. He pulled out his own gun, thinking it was unloaded, and pulled the trigger. The gun fired and wounded Vallandigham, but the lawyer had proved his point. McGehan was set free. Vallandigham was not so lucky—he died of his injuries.

☠ Famous bourbon whiskey-maker Jack Daniel kicked his metal safe in anger when he failed to open it. His toe became infected and the infection spread, killing him in 1911.

☠ In 207 BCE, ancient Greek philosopher Chrysippus died. There are several stories about this. One says he got his donkey drunk and died of laughing as it tried to eat figs.

DANGER AT WORK

Some jobs turn out to be more gory, gruesome, or downright dangerous than others.

Archbishop

A quiet, safe, indoor job? Not if you were an archbishop in Russia in the 16th century with Ivan the Terrible on the throne. It is said that in 1570, Archbishop Pimen of Novgorod was sewn into a bearskin and killed by a pack of hunting dogs.

Wife of a Sultan

A life of luxury and glamour? Perhaps, but the 280 wives of Sultan Ibrahim I all suffered the same fate. They were each tied in a weighted sack and thrown into the River Bosphorus. It's a deep river, and not one of them survived.

Astronomer

Quiet work at night—a safe bet, surely? Not for Hsi and Ho, two ancient Chinese astronomers. They failed to predict a solar eclipse in the 22nd century BCE and were beheaded on the orders of Emperor Chung K'ang.

Servant to a Queen

Protected by palace guards, surely a safe situation? Not if Egyptian Cleopatra was the queen in question. She researched poisons by testing them on prisoners who had been sentenced to death. When she decided to commit suicide by a poisonous snakebite, some of her servants were also ordered to kill themselves or face execution!

OH NO, YOUR MAJESTY, I COULDN'T GO BEFORE YOU!

The Top Job

So maybe the only safe job is the one at the top—ruler. Well, not necessarily. In 2011, a Cambridge University professor studied the lives and deaths of 1,513 European rulers between 600 and 1800 and discovered that almost a quarter of them died violently, mostly by being murdered.

BEWARE! DANGER OF DEATH

There are thousands of rules and regulations to help us keep safe from deadly accidents. Here are some warnings that maybe *should* have been given.

Beware Boomerang Chocolates!

Christiana Edmunds repeatedly bought chocolates from a shop in Brighton, England, laced them with strychnine poison, then returned them to the shop. Didn't anyone think this was odd? Many people became seriously ill, and a four-year-old boy died. Edmunds went on trial in 1872 and was sent to a lunatic asylum for the rest of her life.

OH, MISS EDMUNDS, DIDN'T YOU LIKE THESE ONES EITHER?

YOU CAN'T WEAR THESE. THEY'RE A HEALTH HAZARD.

Always Wear Your Socks!

Calvin Coolidge Jr., the 15-year-old son of President Calvin Coolidge, played tennis with his brother in June 1924. His tennis shoes, worn without socks, gave him a blister, which within days became infected. He died of blood poisoning eight days after the tennis match.

KILLER HISTORY

Be Careful Who You Marry!

In 17th-century Rome, fortune-teller Hieronyma Spara formed a secret organization to help women poison their wealthy husbands with arsenic and inherit their money. She was eventually caught and hanged.

Don't Dangle While Driving!

Isadora Duncan was a dancer who liked to be daring and dramatic. In 1927, she climbed into an open-topped car and, over-the-top as always, she waved good-bye with the words, "Farewell, my friends! I go to glory!" Seconds later, she died when her long scarf became caught in the wheel and broke her neck.

Poetry Can Be Perilous!

According to legend, ancient Chinese poet Li Bai (also known as Li Po) fell from his boat and drowned in the Yangtze River in 762 CE while trying to embrace and kiss the beautiful reflection of the moon in the water.

POISON PLOTS THROUGH THE AGES

Well, Well, Well

Some sneaky ancient Greeks who were attacking the town of Kirra in around 590 BCE poisoned wells that supplied the town with water. They used a poisonous plant, the hellebore. The Kirrans became so ill that they were easy to defeat.

The ancient Assyrians used a fungus called ergot to poison enemy wells in the 6th century BCE. The fungus could cause people to suffer hallucinations and die.

The Problem with Poison

Mithridates VI was the ruler of a kingdom in northern Turkey. He was so afraid of plots to poison him that he

started taking an antidote every day to try to make himself immune.

When defeated by the Romans in 63 BCE, he foolishly tried to commit suicide by taking poison. Needless to say, he failed. He had to force one of his own soldiers to kill him instead.

TOILET TROUBLE

I THINK I'LL USE ANOTHER BATHROOM!

According to legend, King Edmund II of England was murdered in 1016 when his attacker hid in the toilet below him and stabbed him with either a dagger or sharpened wooden pole. Ouch!

George II, a much later king of England, died from a blood vessel rupture while in the bathroom and either sitting on the toilet or falling off it—no one is certain—in 1760.

Roman emperor Caracalla was stabbed to death with a sword in 217 CE, after he had dismounted his horse to go pee.

CREEPY CORPSE

Giovanni Aldini electrified onlookers in 1803 when he made the corpse of a dead murderer, George Forster, seemingly come back to life. Aldini had connected the body to a 120-volt battery, and Forster's fist clenched, his legs kicked about, and his jaw quivered. Very few people had seen electricity in action before.

Aldini's eerie experiment may have been in Mary Shelley's mind 12 years later when she began to write *Frankenstein*.

STICKY ENDS

Poking a pole or spear through a body part is called impaling. Over the years, many different people seem to have found the idea appealing.

☠ Around 3,000 years ago, parents of children who died in northern Scotland carried their remains to Sculptor's Cave near Lossiemouth. Many of the children's heads were placed on sticks in the cave, which can only be reached at low tide.

☠ Seventeenth-century English leader Oliver Cromwell died of natural causes in 1658, but three years later, his body was dug up and hanged as a traitor. His head was cut off and placed on a spike outside Westminster Hall, where it stayed for around 20 years.

☠ Native American chief Metacomet was executed in 1676 by European settlers. His head was displayed on a stick in Plymouth, Massachusetts, for around 20 years.

KILLER HISTORY

☠ Vlad III Dracul, prince of Wallachia (1431–1476), is sometimes called Vlad the Impaler. No wonder! He was known for killing people in nasty ways and particularly liked impaling their bodies on sticks to scare off enemies. His dark deeds may have been what inspired Bram Stoker to write the ultimate vampire story—*Dracula*.

MACABRE MUSEUM

The Musée Fragonard is a museum in Paris, France, that showcases some of the work of Honoré Fragonard. He made models using dead animals and people that had been skinned and posed in different positions. One of his most famous is *The Horseman of the Apocalypse*—a skinned dead man riding a skinned dead horse.

FATAL FIRSTS

1785: First Balloon Death

Jean-François Pilâtre de Rozier had two ballooning firsts. He became the first hot-air balloonist when he piloted the Montgolfier brothers' balloon in 1783. Two years later, he became the first balloonist to die as he tried to fly across the English Channel.

IS IT ME, OR IS IT GETTING SMALLER?

1830: First Railroad Death

William Huskisson was a member of British Parliament and a guest at the opening of the Manchester to Liverpool railroad line. Unfortunately, he fell under the train's wheels and died nine hours later.

POOR GUY DIDN'T STAND A CHANCE. IT MUST HAVE BEEN DOING AT LEAST 3 MPH.

1869: First Car Death

Irishwoman Mary Ward fell from a steam-powered car built by her cousins and broke her neck.

THEY OUGHT TO DO SOMETHING ABOUT THESE BUMPS!

1890: First Death by Electric Chair
William Kemmler, convicted of the axe murder of his girlfriend Matilda Ziegler, became the first person to be executed by electric chair, at Auburn Prison in New York.

1904: First Death from Radiation
Clarence Madison Dally, an assistant of the great inventor Thomas Edison, experimented with extremely powerful X-rays. His hair and mustache fell out and both his arms were so damaged they had to be amputated. He later died of cancer caused by radiation.

1908: First Aircraft Passenger Death
Orville Wright was the first person to fly in a powered plane in 1903. Five years later, he was performing a test flight with a passenger, Lieutenant Thomas Selfridge, when the plane lost control and nose-dived almost 80 feet (25 meters) to the ground. Wright survived, but his passenger did not.

ASHES TO FLASHES

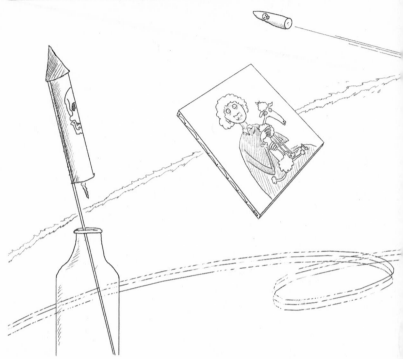

After cremation, your ashes can be buried . . . or they can be turned into something spectacular.

☠ Marvel Comics writer Mark Gruenwald's last request was for his ashes to be mixed with ink and the mixture used to print comic books. He got his wish and became part of a comic called *Squadron Supreme*.

☠ An American company takes just over 1 pound (500 grams) of cremated ashes and makes 250 bullets with them. Loved ones can then fire them out of rifles, shotguns, or other weapons.

☠ A fireworks company will put a cremated person's ashes into four or more rockets for a sparkling display.

☠ An artist in the US produces portraits of dead people and pets with some of their ashes mixed into the paints.

☠ Another company will heat cremated ashes or a lock of hair under pressure and create an artificial diamond.

☠ The ashes of Ed Headrick, who pioneered the Frisbee, were mixed with plastic and used to make a limited edition memorial Frisbee.

DIY MUMMIFICATION

When the ancient Egyptians made mummies (see page 12), they began by removing the body's insides, as they would be the first to decompose (rot). Scientists were astonished to find that some mummies in Japan still had their internal organs. The reason? These were Buddhist monks who had mummified themselves while they were still alive!

Here's how they did it:

1. For 1,000 days, the monk ate only seeds and nuts. He became very thin. The idea was to get rid of body fat, which was known to decompose quickly after death.

EWWW! DON'T EAT THAT ONE!

2. For the next 1,000 days, the monk ate only little bits of pine-tree bark and roots. Toward the end of this time, he started drinking a special tea made from the urushi tree. It was a poison that made the monk very ill, but it also meant that his whole body was poisonous, and insects wouldn't want to eat it after death.

3. In the last stage, the monk, just skin and bones and very near death, was put in an underground tomb. He was given a bell and a straw to breathe through. Each day, the monk rang the bell. When the tomb was silent, his fellow monks knew he was dead and sealed up the breathing hole.

4. Then, 1,000 days later, the other monks opened the tomb. Most of the time they found skeletons. Occasionally, they found a mummified body, which was then dressed in fine clothes and put in a shrine to be worshipped. They believed the monk had succeeded in becoming one with the Buddha and was very holy.

SO YOU THINK YOU KNOW A ZOMBIE?

A zombie is a dead person who has been revived by magic, voodoo, or witchcraft after burial. Sometimes zombies are known as the "undead," but fortunately they only appear in horror movies and comics. However, if you suspect any of your friends of being zombies, here are ten telltale signs to look out for.

1. They stop eating salad and vegetables and start threatening to eat human brains.

2. Their skin becomes paler than usual.

3. They walk with a slow shuffle (okay, many teenagers do this, but even slower and more shuffly than usual).

4. They have the second Saturday in October—World Zombie Day—circled on their calendars.

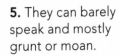

5. They can barely speak and mostly grunt or moan.

6. They have bite marks on their skin that are infected. This is the possible cause of their zombie-dom.

7. They rarely brush their teeth or use deodorant, and they smell awful.

8. They are unable to do puzzles, crosswords, or other tasks that require brain power.

9. They don't sleep at all.

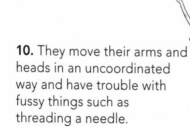

10. They move their arms and heads in an uncoordinated way and have trouble with fussy things such as threading a needle.

KILLER HISTORY

MAKE YOUR OWN BREAD OF THE DEAD

Pan de muerto, or "bread of the dead," is a sweet, doughy bread flavored with orange, which is traditionally made on November 1 for the Mexican Day of the Dead festival (see page 78). Here's how to make some Bread of the Dead rolls for you to enjoy all year round. This recipe makes seven tasty bread rolls.

You Will Need:

- ¼ cup (60 milliliters) milk • ½ stick butter (60 grams)
- ¼ cup (60 milliliters) warm water plus a little extra for sprinkling • 2⅔ cups (400 grams) white bread flour plus extra for kneading • 3 teaspoons (8 grams) baker's yeast
- ⅓ cup (75 grams) powdered sugar • 2 eggs (beaten)
- zest of 1 orange (finely grated) • 2 teaspoons aniseeds.

Warning: Ask an adult to help you when using the stove.

1. In a saucepan, heat the milk and butter until they are melted and combined. Then add the warm water and leave to cool down to a lukewarm temperature.

2. Mix ⅔ cups (100 grams) of the flour with all of the yeast and the sugar in a large mixing bowl. Add the butter, milk, and water mixture, the eggs, orange zest, and aniseeds.

3. Stir, then add the remaining flour and use your hands to mix it all together until a soft dough forms.

4. Put the dough on to a lightly floured surface. Use the heel of your hand to push into the dough, then stretch it back on itself before pushing into it again. Do this for about a minute.

5. Place the dough back in the mixing bowl, cover it with a clean towel, and leave it to rise for 90 minutes.

6. Put the risen dough on a floured surface, and use your fingertips to push the air out of it.

7. Split the dough into eight equal-size portions, and shape seven of them into round rolls.

8. Break off little bits of the eighth piece of dough and roll them into thin sausage shapes and small balls between your hands. You need to get fourteen thin sausages and seven small balls of dough from this piece.

9. Sprinkle the rolls with a few drops of water, then lay two sausage shapes crossways over the top of each one, and top them with a small ball of dough. These are the bones for the bread of the dead.

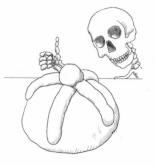

10. Leave the rolls to rise again for an hour, then bake them in a preheated oven (350°F/180°C) for 20 minutes until golden.

Top Tip. Ask an adult to heat the juice of half an orange with 5 teaspoons (25 grams) powdered sugar until the sugar has dissolved. Brush this sweet glaze over your rolls for a truly tasty finish.

CANNIBALS!

Eating dead humans seems horrible to most of us, but some people take a different view.

Family Feast
The Wari tribe from the Amazon rainforest used to practice cannibalism on members of their own people. When a wife died, members of the husband's family would feast on her remains. When the Wari first had contact with European and modern South American customs, they were horrified by the idea of burying a dead loved one in the cold, dirty earth.

Eating the Enemy

French sailor Joseph Kabris lived with a cannibal tribe on the Pacific island of Nuku Hiva between 1796 and 1804. He reported that in times of war and famine, prisoners seized after battles were eaten. It seems the eyes, cheeks, and brains were the favorite parts.

Dine or Die

Some people have resorted to cannibalism in order to survive in extreme situations. Four sailors were marooned in a lifeboat in the Indian Ocean after their yacht, the *Mignonette*, sank in 1884. After 19 days at sea, two of the sailors killed the youngest, a cabin boy called Parker, and ate parts of him to survive. They were rescued some days later.

DEATH DEFEATED

Some people have made amazing recoveries when it seemed that death was the only outcome.

Firing Squad Fiasco

Wenseslao Moguel was sentenced to death by firing squad during the Mexican Revolution of 1915. He was shot a total of nine times by the gunmen but amazingly was still alive. He pretended to be dead and managed to escape when the firing squad left.

EXCUSE ME, I'M OVER HERE!

Defrosted

In 1985, a two-year-old boy, Michael Troche, was found frozen stiff in sub-zero temperatures in Milwaukee, Wisconsin. He had stopped breathing, ice crystals had formed under his skin, and a doctor pronounced him dead. Yet Michael eventually came around and made an amazing recovery.

A Narrow Escape

Magan Kanwar, a 72-year-old woman from Jaipur, India, was declared dead from a blood clot and was about to have her body burned on a funeral pyre when she was found to be breathing.

Happy Landings

Juliane Koepcke was on board an aircraft struck by lightning in 1971. The lightning ripped the plane apart and killed all 92 passengers and crew, except 17-year-old Juliane, who fell, strapped in her seat, almost 2 miles (3,000 meters) before crashing into the Amazon rainforest. In shock, with broken bones, no food, and infections from insect bites, she walked for nine days through the jungle before being rescued and recovering fully.

DEATH TO SPIES

Being a spy can be a dangerous career choice. When a spy gets caught, things might well turn deadly.

Losing Her Head
Legendary female spy Mata Hari (real name Margaretha Zelle) was killed by firing squad. She was executed in 1917 by French forces, after being found guilty of spying for the Germans during World War I. Her body was not claimed by family members, and for a while her embalmed head was stored in the Museum of Anatomy in Paris.

Death Choice
During the American Revolutionary War, British spy John André was caught and sentenced to death. He pleaded with General George Washington, not for a pardon but to be killed by firing squad instead of hanging. His request was refused, and he was hanged in 1780.

SMERSH

In the 1940s, the Soviet Union had an organization that aimed to root out foreign spies and disloyal soldiers in its own armies, often torturing and sometimes killing them if found. The organization was known as SMERSH, from the Russian phrase *smert shpionam,* which means "death to spies."

Killing Coin

Some American spies in the 20th century were equipped with a "dollar of death." It looked like an ordinary coin, but it was hollow. Inside was either a tiny pill or a pin tipped with lethal poison. If he or she was captured, the spy often faced torture, as the captors tried to find out what the spy knew. The coin gave the spy the choice of suicide instead.

DEADLY DOCTORS

In the past, some medical methods made going to the doctor distinctly dangerous.

You Need This Like a Hole in the Head!

In some ancient civilizations, a bad headache was sometimes treated by giving you an even worse one. "Trepanning" is the medical practice of making a hole in a patient's skull.

Nowadays, doctors know that relieving pressure after a head injury may actually be a good idea, but long ago the operation was done with rough tools and no pain-numbing drugs. Many patients must have died. The amazing thing is that some did not. Skulls have been found in which the wounds had begun to heal.

Blood Loss

For more than 3,000 years, doctors thought that patients might be made better by losing blood! Bloodletting, as it was known, was done by cutting into a vein with a knife. There was a danger of the wound becoming infected, and after several sessions, some patients lost so much blood that they died anyway.

Asleep . . . Forever

Until the 19th century, there was no general anesthetic to make patients unconscious before an operation. Sleeping remedies were used, but most didn't work well and some were really deadly. A recipe from an Italian monastery in the year 800 included lettuce juice, mulberry juice, ivy, opium, henbane, and hemlock. Those last three plants are deadly poisons!

BLOODSTAIN BUSINESS

A Scottish doctor named John Glaister (1892–1971) felt that more could be learned from bloodstains if they could be grouped and described. He suggested six different kinds of bloodstain, which could help investigators find out more about how deaths had occured.

☠ Drops on a horizontal surface, such as a floor or table

☠ Splashes, from blood flying through the air and hitting a surface at an angle

☠ Pools around the body

☠ Smears left by a bleeding person moving

☠ Spurts from a major blood vessel

☠ Trails of blood from a body being carried or dragged

KILLER HISTORY

MISSING AND PRESUMED DEAD

Sometimes, people seem to vanish without a trace, and no dead body is ever found. Here are some of the most mysterious missing persons.

WELL, WE'VE TRACED FAWCETT'S EXPEDITION TO HERE. NOW WHAT?

☠ Famous explorer Percy Fawcett and his expedition disappeared in 1925 while searching for a fabled ancient city in the rainforests of Brazil. More than a hundred people have died searching for Fawcett and his team.

☠ Amelia Earhart, a famous female pilot, disappeared in 1937 over the Pacific Ocean, while flying her *Lockheed Electra* aircraft. No conclusive evidence of the plane or Earhart have been recovered.

☠ Australian prime minister Harold Holt was a strong swimmer, yet he disappeared off Cheviot Beach, Australia, in 1967. His body was never found.

☠ Richard Bingham, 7th Earl of Lucan, known as Lord Lucan, disappeared in 1974, after his children's nanny was found dead at his home in London, England.

FATAL FLOODS

Beer!

The London Beer Flood of 1814 sounds as if it might have been fun for adults, but when tanks at a brewery on Tottenham Court Road burst, more than 200,000 gallons (more than one million liters) of beer flooded the street, killing at least nine people.

Molasses!

The Great Boston Molasses Flood occurred in 1919. Massive waves of molasses (a thick, dark, sugary syrup) flowed at speeds around 35 mph (more than 50 km/h) after a giant storage tank broke. Around 21 people met a particularly sticky end.

BOILING BODIES

In 1531, King Henry VIII of England made boiling in water a punishment for people found guilty of poisoning. The bishop of Rochester's cook, who poisoned two people, was boiled to death the following year. The last person to be executed in Britain by boiling was a maid called Margaret Davy in 1542.

In the 15th century, people who forged money in the Dutch town of Deventer were likely to be boiled alive in oil in a large copper kettle. The kettle is still on display in the town.

Not all guests who checked into the Ostrich Inn in the 17th century checked out alive. The owner of the hotel in Colnbrook, just west of London, England, had a trapdoor installed in the inn's best guest room. The trapdoor would drop a guest straight into a cauldron of boiling water in the kitchens below, allowing the innkeeper to steal all his belongings.

HMMM. A LITTLE MORE SALT, I THINK.

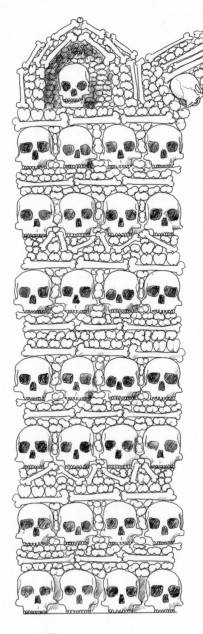

INFAMOUS OSSUARIES

An "ossuary" is a place where bones are kept. Here are five extraordinary ones.

1. The *Capela dos Ossos* is a chapel in Evora, Portugal. It's decorated inside with the skulls and bones of about 5,000 dead people, mostly monks.

2. The Skull Chapel in Czermna, Poland, contains the skulls of some 3,000 dead people in its walls, with hundreds of shin bones making up the ceiling. And that's not all. In the cellar below the small chapel can be found a further 21,000 human skulls.

3. In the Spanish village of Wamba, the Church of Santa Maria contains organized piles of around 1,000 skulls of local people who died between the 12th and 18th centuries.

4. Sedlec Ossuary in the Czech Republic contains the bony remains of more than 40,000 people. Many of their bones have been fashioned into furniture and decorations. These include a giant chandelier containing at least one of every bone in the human body. It has to be the weirdest light fixture in the world.

5. The biggest hoard of bones in Europe can be found in Paris. The Catacombs of Paris contain more than 186 miles (300 kilometers) of tunnels, in which lie the bones of six million people. The bones were moved there from the 1780s onward because of a lack of space for cemeteries and burial plots in the city.

FASCINATING FUNERALS

Some cultures deal with their dead in interesting ways. Read on to find out more.

☠ The Toraja people, who live on the Indonesian island of Sulawesi, kill water buffalo when a person dies. The more important the person, the longer the funeral lasts and the more animals are sacrificed.

☠ In the past, the Toraja used to bury babies who died inside the trunks of living trees, believing that the child might continue to grow with the tree.

☠ The Bo people of southwest China used a coffin to hold a dead body but then hung the coffin over the edge of a steep cliff. The coffin stayed there as long as the ropes used to lower it lasted.

☠ In Tibet, *jhator*—"sky burial"—is still practiced by some followers of Buddhism. A dead person's body is left out in the open for a few days, cleaned, and then broken and cut into a number of pieces so that it can be eaten by wild creatures.

☠ Zoroastrians are followers of a religion that began in ancient Iran around 3,500 years ago. They believe that when a body dies, it is unclean, so it is placed on a structure called a *dokhma*, or "tower of silence," in the open air. There the body is exposed to the sun and eaten by birds of prey.

☠ In the past, when some Hindu men died, their wives would perform *suttee* (or *sati*). When the husband's body was burned on a funeral pyre, the wife would join him and would be burned alive. *Suttee* was never widely practiced and was made illegal in 1829, but a few cases have happened since.

☠ Many ancient Mayan people of Central America buried their relatives under their homes, along with their favorite tools and objects. People were often buried with maize cereal in their mouths to provide them with food for their "life" after death.

DEATHS IN THE WILD WEST

It was known as the land of cowboys, outlaws, and gunslingers, so it's no surprise that the Wild West became infamous for a few well-known deaths.

☠ John Wesley Hardin was a notorious Wild West gunfighter who killed between 27 and 42 men before being sent to prison. Hardin was eventually shot and killed in 1895 by another gunman, John Selman, while playing dice in the Acme Saloon in El Paso, Texas.

☠ While playing poker in a saloon in Deadwood, South Dakota, famous gunslinger James "Wild Bill" Hickok was shot dead from behind by Jack McCall. As he fell, the playing cards he was holding were the ace of clubs, the ace of spades, and a pair of eights. This is known to this day as the "Dead Man's Hand."

☠ In 1891, an infamous gunfight broke out near the OK Corral in the mining town of Tombstone, Arizona. It lasted less than a minute, but the brothers Wyatt, Virgil, and Morgan Earp and their pal, gunslinger Doc Holliday, killed three men. The men were buried at Boot Hill Cemetery—so named because many of those buried there died sudden, violent deaths . . . with their boots on.

☠ Not all famous gunfighters died at the hands of others. William Sidney Light, a former deputy sheriff turned criminal, accidentally shot himself when riding on a train in 1893. He pulled the trigger of the gun in his pocket by mistake, shooting a large hole in his leg. He died of massive blood loss shortly afterwards.

☠ George Parrott, also known as Big Nose George, was an outlaw from Wyoming. He was arrested and executed for the murder of two law enforcers, but his story doesn't end there. The doctor examining his corpse after execution had George's skin stripped from his body and made into shoes, which he wore for several years afterward. Now that's some frightful footwear!

DREADFULLY DEADLY DEFINITIONS

Amputate
To cut off an injured or infected body part.

Assassin
Someone who kills an important person in a surprise attack.

Bequeath
To pass on something via a will.

Buboes
Painful swollen lumps around the armpits and groin. A symptom of the Bubonic Plague.

Capital Punishment
The legal execution of people convicted of crimes.

Catacomb
An underground cemetery.

Cemetery
A place where bodies are taken to be buried.

Corpse
A dead body.

Cremation
Burning a dead body to ashes.

Deceased
Dead.

Decomposition
The breaking down of a body after death, often causing a bad smell.

DNA
A set of instructions found in all living things, which tells them how to function.

Epidemic
A widespread illness or infection.

Execution
A legal killing intended to punish.

Exhumation
The process of digging up a buried body.

Forensic Pathologist
Someone who examines dead bodies to find out how they died.

Funeral Pyre
A pile of wood or other material that burns on which a body is laid and set fire to as part of a funeral rite.

Gangrene
A condition in which tissue in the body dies due to lack of bloodflow.

Mace
A large club with spikes on the end of it, used as a weapon.

Mourning
Grieving for someone who has recently died.

Murder
The deliberate killing of someone else.

Noose
A loop of rope placed around the neck of someone being hanged.

Sacrifice
A person or an animal who is killed as an offering.

Suicide
The deliberate killing of oneself.

INDEX

Reader's Digest Books for Young Readers

I Wish I Knew That

This fun and engaging book will give young readers a jump start on everything from art, music, literature, and ancient myths to history, geography, science, and math.

STEVE MARTIN, DR. MIKE GOLDSMITH, AND MARIANNE TAYLOR
978-1-60652-340-7

Liar! Liar! Pants on Fire!

Sometimes the truth can be so strange that it's hard to believe. With hundreds of incredible true—and false—questions, kids have a great time testing their knowledge, learning fascinating truths, and uncovering lousy lies!

JAN PAYNE • 978-1-60652-476-3

Write (Or Is That "Right"?) Every Time

Divided into bite-size chunks that include Goodness Gracious Grammar, Spelling Made Simple, and Punctuation Perfection, this book provides quick-and-easy tips and tricks to overcome every grammar challenge.

LOTTIE STRIDE • 978-1-60652-341-4

Out of This World

Are you baffled by the Big Bang? Curious about what it's like to walk on the moon? Bursting with intergalactic information, this book gives you everything you need to know about space, from the Earth's atmosphere to the edge of the universe.

CLIVE GIFFORD • 978-1-60652-519-7

Other Titles Available in This Series